# Surreal Expulsion

D. R. James

A Publication of The Poetry Box®

©2019 D. R. James
All rights reserved.

Editing & Book Design by Shawn Aveningo Sanders
Cover Design by Robert R. Sanders
Original Cover Art: "Pink Topography" by Meridith Ridl
Author photo by Suzy Doyle

No part of this book may be reproduced in any manner whatsoever without permission from the author, except in the case of brief quotations embodied in critical essays, reviews and articles.

ISBN: 978-1-948461-24-5
Printed in the United States of America.

Published by The Poetry Box®, 2019
Beaverton, Oregon
ThePoetryBox.com

*To all the victims of gun and military violence throughout the world, especially the far too many young people murdered, maimed, and traumatized in, of all places, their schools.*

# Contents

## — I —

| | |
|---|---|
| New Year Cliché'd | 9 |
| Upon Recognizing that Yesterday's 'Well-Meaning' Poem Was Still as Paternalistic as Ever | 10 |
| The 27th of January, 2017 | 11 |
| Lines Concocted While Waiting to Catch a Certain Bent Blue Note in Jimi Hendrix's Second Guitar Solo of "Voodoo Child (Slight Return)" Recorded Live at London's Albert Hall, February 24, 1969 | 12 |
| Brit Lit Weighs In | 14 |
| OK, Here's What We Do: An Allegory | 16 |

## — II —

| | |
|---|---|
| Penny | 19 |
| Free Ride | 20 |
| A – maze – d | 21 |
| Dream at Wits' End | 22 |
| Wedged, Continued | 23 |

## — III —

| | |
|---|---|
| Imagining a Demise | 27 |
| First Light | 28 |
| Pain, No Gain | 29 |
| An Assembly of God | 31 |
| Pope Goes, a Weasel? | 32 |
| April 15, 2013 | 34 |
| Make a Difference! | 35 |
| Surreal Expulsion | 36 |

*  *  *

| | |
|---|---|
| Notes | 39 |
| Acknowledgments | 41 |
| Praise for *Surreal Expulsion* | 43 |
| About the Author | 45 |
| About The Poetry Box® | 47 |

– I –

# New Year Cliché'd
## *~ January 1, 2017*

That kind of title for one, to mark
this particular *año nuevo* like that for another,
to be going on in this vein yet another.
Too metta?
Meh: it's all
contradictory cringing:
ashes outing a vicious victory:
archetypal exile among the flood of smudged hours:
barbarity, barrels of it:
unity like underwater faces facing the eternal stones:
novel remnants reaching their only sub-zero:
rank antagonism anti-brave and shackled
ardent to a cannon sprouted and ever-violating:
a personal-as-political-pilgrimaged sacred labor
to dismantle the sprawling urban-cowboy threat.
Instead, to self-possess:
still-woods light slanting certainly:
light snow grounded like disbanding fondant:
isolated leaves left dissed, connected, oscillating beiges:
lines bearing on (comes the tardy turn!):
"at this time last year, next year:
ziplocked thoughts extolling totems totally devoted to X."

# Upon Recognizing Yesterday's 'Well-Meaning' Poem Was Still as Paternalistic as Ever
## —1/22/17

Outside, still January, but 40 not 15,
gauzy, black-and-white woods
from *The Wolf Man.* Inside,
a gauzy-gray (un?)consciousness
from *This White Man,* half-reclined
in buttery, dove-gray leather. It's envisioning
millions of protesting women, now back
perhaps in their individual towns,
their power *proclaimed* not awakened,
or still making their way back
from D.C., G.R., L.A., NYC,
Denver, Chicago, Baltimore,
Honolulu, Madison, Wichita,
Reno, Boston, Memphis, Atlanta,
Albuquerque, Gulfport, Asbury Park,
Laramie, Ashville, Orlando, Seattle,
Old Saybrook, Corpus Christie, Erie, Roanoke,
Eugene, New Delhi, Vienna, Minsk,
La Paz, Prague, Strasbourg, Botswana,
EX Village des Jeux Ankorondrano,
Dublin, Athens, San Jose, Sofia,
Copenhagen, Tel Aviv, Geneva, Liverpool,
Cape Town, Moscow, Yellow Knife, Beirut,
Buenos Aires, Belgrade, Bangkok, Boise….
Will it never, ever learn?

# The 27ᵗʰ of January, 2017
### —after Kinnel

A Friday (day of Frigg,
Norse goddess of wisdom)
that sags gray as brains.
The day closing the long week
since a certain absurdity
began to un-settle itself in—
(blurting like boils from under
maize-ish, cirrocumular mesh,
ranting, being ranted, mouthing
black smoke, inhaling black hearts,
splaying deal-breakers like pollutants
burping out over America First factories,
self-deluding in centrifugal elipticals)—
continues. And a four-year
interim begins: protest marches,
opinion polls, endless petitions,
reorganizations, reactions,
confrontations, wiser fights,
phone calls, letter blitzes—but also
through-it-all candid accord?

# Lines Concocted While Waiting to Catch a Certain Bent Blue Note in Jimi Hendrix's Second Guitar Solo of "Voodoo Child (Slight Return)" Recorded Live at London's Albert Hall, February 24, 1969

Anything could happen this winter
in the frail rise and fall,
the lonely moans, of a landscape
no longer muscly with growth.

To start something new
will require a sort of slackening,
a giving way when the knife of wind
takes its first and second swipes
and the low-slung sun
paints a neon sky, rays
oozing around clouds in a hurry.

The blackened limb above the porch will sport
its sculpted snow boa, puffed fuselage
for the butterfly of spring.

Those hawks who recently mounted high thermals
over fields now gone all-brown
will send love from Guatemala.

The attic will reclaim
the decorations I'm to cart there.

And optimism will seem a stretch—

like when pristine stone won't detonate.

# Brit Lit Weighs In
*(a cento)*

Billows were breaking, sea against sand,
long before prime had rung from any bell—
and from a long way, hard and dangerous.
Yet little good hath got, and much lesse gayne
by spells and medicines bought of mountebanks.
Each flower had wept, and bowed toward the east,
time's winged chariot hurrying near,
but when the assault was intended to the city,
(before polygamy was made a sin)
their fluid bodies half dissolved in the light.
Cruel with guilt, and daring with despair,
the applause of listening senates to command,
they reeled, they set, they crossed, they cleekit,
and then the perilous path was planted.
I rose and turned toward a group of trees
through caverns measureless to man,
which kept my optics free from all delusion,
now dark—now glittering—now reflecting gloom—
diffused unseen throughout eternal space.
Once more uprose the mystic mountain-range,
and I, perchance, half felt a strange regret
of all the thousand nothings of the hour,
not knowing in any wise compassion,
all things counter, original, spare, strange.
Drawn on by vague imaginings, maybe,
the full round moon and the star-laden sky,
to wonder, 'Do I dare?' and, 'Do I dare?'
tell me not here, it needs not saying.

This land, cut off, will not communicate:
spot the blown word, and on the seas I imagine,
in short, a past that no one now can share.

# OK, Here's What We Do: An Allegory

Well, we enlarge the grown-up table for
the far-flung fragments of our Family.
Here's our current Winter spent in agony,
here's our disrespected Sister, here is War
that mushrooms undiminished, glibly tears
our global Soul to slivers. And here We are;
and here's a Brute beside us so bizarre
that nearly nothing else we've known compares—
as if we'd acceded to some greater Hell.
Ah, but here's what's left of human Dignity.
Seated here's Resolve to trample Travesty.
But there's our Greatest Fear that's hard to quell....
Hey, this isn't fatalistic Falderal!
We must make sure the table's set for All.

– II –

# Penny

The b & w photo, not posed, is the picture of 50's innocence: little boy, five, with a butch and sensible shoes, little bow tie, little vest over crisp white shirt. Sitting 'Indian' style, he pets his little dog, who no kidding lies at his knee looking adoringly over her shoulder and up into his grinning face. Behind them and outside the picture-perfect picture window, the rear end of a two-toned coupe (gray and white in the photo and, if memory serves, reality), but stock, that is, not souped-up like it might be ten years later, by then the famous '57 Chevy favored by hot-rodders when the boy would be turning fifteen. Like all photos, this one doesn't show it all. Not the half of it. Not most of why it's made its way into this confession. It leaves out how the small-bodied boy finds it easy to overpower the little dog, cower her with his angry-albeit-little-boy voice, threatening to slap her until he switches abruptly to cooing just to see the relief spread from nervous face through trembling body to tail curled between her legs. It leaves out how his parents will put her down while he's away at camp. It leaves out how instead of 'predicating a tendency toward social pathology,' this history merely marks an eccentric twisting in the inexplicable path.

# Free Ride

Yoda-like—the eyes, the smile, even the ears that flume from under a pinstriped engineer's cap—the tiny man-boy careens around Sweet Pea's Espresso, serene and squat and centered in a chair as solid as a forklift. With every turn, every flick of his right-hand joystick, he threatens a chair leg, a top-heavy double latte, a stockinged shin, a disgusted look. His parents, Barbie and Ken, sit nursing cappuccinos, bribing his little sister with a bagel and pink-flavored cream cheese. Already a giant to her older brother, she will one day be as precious as her mommy. "How about riding in… now, who is this…?" Ken baits the boy across the tabletops and financial sections, pointing to Tommy the Tank Engine installed for toddlers on the tile floor of the old smoking section. The boy pulls up sharp, whirls around. "Yes, I wanna ride him, Daddy!" He circles back, dodging the girl bussing the two- and four-tops, who backs away in a clatter of cups and saucers piled high in her plastic bin. He's a mechanical pigeon, homing in on his hero but honking like Daffy on helium. "Put in the money, Daddy. Lemme ride!" Lifted from its roost by armpits no deeper than divots, his body, seemingly half dead, dangles springy, naked legs like sprung sausage curls that slide easily into Tommy's pilot house. The fit is perfect and, at the clink of a token, the bullish ride, euphoric. The ancient face savors every swirl, every hydraulic spasm. He's Oscar Peterson mumbling at the piano, Bird Parker juking on sax. The convulsive legs never stop jazzing. Meanwhile, Barbie wet-thumbs the corners of their daughter's sticky mouth, the blond wispies at her temples, cooing to the perfect girl straining to witness her big brother's totemic ecstasy.

# A – maze – d

*—after an untitled painting by Merle Rosen*

Dive in anywhere. Go 'round and 'round on pearl or coral, cross on cobalt, stall against the black mass, the black slabs that finger under rivers of rose. Your hazel eyes will search unmirrored the rings like years, the vibrato'd, banded angles. Your sparrow childhood will scan for the far mouth of corn stalks, inflict patient waiting before screaming. Scrawls in clay will cue the silliness of ancient glyphs. Saplings will bend and sing to the wind. Darkened leaves will unhem. Dawn's paradise will shatter, the constellations of fine lines torn apart for a merciless afterward waving like harsh flags. But then a familiar vermillion will send autumn's frost dissolving, the diurnal hours zigzag-falling like freewheeling feathers, until tonight ages into its sedate pitch, those baffling coils slacken into cool-jazz Taps, and you view the horizon: slimmed, glimmered, wobbling.

# Dream at Wits' End

Under branches defying gravity the path meandered toward the nursery. From an uncertain height all eyes seemed upon us. The silence of blossoms made it at first feel right. Leaf-fall, bleeding from selected trees, the greenhouse at its designated distance, argued for the set-up as an outgrowth of nature, the temperature not as a kind of poison. In fact, the caretakers were in league with economies of fear. They would take mallets to our knees. These thorns were gods and we travelers, worshippers, torsos caught eternally in coarse and caustic brambles. What use to mouth inane prayers or stride like animals? What use to side-step the torn stubble like creatures of the night? We'd need streamers of fire to excavate a trench toward home. We'd need to swivel our shoulders, plunge through the forest without helmets, pause before the altar whose namesake was our mother, whose stanchions were of heartwood, whose scene allowed no repeating. Our best intentions undercut before daylight, our balance challenged by the frequency of foxholes, our voices reduced to the capacity of swine, our vision limited like a gas-lit lamp, we ping-ponged till pleading Uncle.

# Wedged, Continued

Some days I even dare face whether the (un)(re)stored fortress of language that bears up my own subtle house of doubts is surfacing or sinking and whether my sentience is like a band of seekers crossing then walking its idyllic beach, drawn by the free music of wind and surf, or like exiles-like-mice left to roast in its thick wilderness of land-locked dunes, the sky scraping and thriving overhead, bordering on ash no matter dawn or attitudinal dusk, no matter the cringe of sun hung low, its scrimmed rise or fall. Other times, the hours like shifting sands penetrating or escaping a weathered perimeter flood with the cowed wonder of what might lie beyond: dark cliffs, remnants eaten away from a tilted world, mythic stones stood and held on edge, a remote ocean boiling away its underwater flora and fauna. Or just maybe mind's way one day will move easily like wheels over a hard but ebbing frost, eventually barreling down the clean slopes with the look and smell of lucidity borne of speed—but all caught still in the taut ebullience of sapient insufficiency.

– III –

# Imagining a Demise
### —*after Neruda*

A profile like a pasty corpse robed
in silk pajamas inside 'the home,'
the laughter like ashes in their ring,
the psalm of grief hovering like a period,
the calm shadowy fraud,
the jokes, the riddles, the emergency
moans buttoned into blind lounges,
the waterfalls singing of the grass, the gory gray ocean
breathed from below, from a quaking basement:
all late-middle-agings, conveying and lurching
like barks blown away in the wind.

# First Light

After the year of mere staring,
various grays at last color
tree, beach, breaker, the dark

undersides of waves, textured seas
arriving gently from an even,
medium gray. The horizon,

barely reckoned, smoothed
to its worn sheen, intersects
inexpressive sky, sedate Great Lake,

flattened and diaphanous—
like the road-show backdrop
before which one might finally

enact the refurbishment
of a feeble—no, make that
a threadbare—life.

# Pain, No Gain

Inflexibility restricts
range of motion &
energy transfer. Always
warm up; always
lengthen. If tight,
stop to stretch, rest,
rehydrate, reduce
the possibility of injury.
Wrong way or wrong
time tightens rather
than relaxes. The old
"bounce, bounce, bounces"
risk small tears &
are not recommended.

The stretch reflex responds
to voluntary movement:
the spindles initiating
their counter contraction;
the Golgi organ,
given twenty seconds,
relaxing the muscle
and its counter muscle
in response. Thus stretch
only to a slight pull, slight
discomfort, hold-

relax. Fool
the reflex, activate
the organ. Stretching

will differ per individual.
Stretching is not competitive.
Stretching should never involve pain.

# An Assembly of God

This church—now calm across its watered lawn—
whose congregants, kneeling or lining pews,
mutter, meditate, and meekly altar-fawn

before the bellied, brimstoning minister,
is never brief, always loud in offering song
each Sunday, every Wednesday, in the stir

of summer's open-windowed air. They dote,
you'll notice, upon his every whim, his stern
commands to trim the hedges, layer on coats

of driveway tar, repair the shutters, and
mow the manse's grass like servile goats.
Even boys in bunches shovel gutter sand.

But look! A lacy little girl in shiny shoes
comes fluttering among the unsung mothers and,
still young, postpones payment of her fated dues.

# Pope Goes, a Weasel?

Six hundred years!
A pretty good hiatus as
abdicationing goes.

It doesn't take amnesia
not to know an *anti*pope
dispatched the last.

Before that, a flip-flop
every half-century or so.
Some can't stomach— or

can! —such rotten fish, can't
face the filthy task of filtering
the good from bad, the grit

from the humid air of
human fare, of running block
before a scam can spring

to light. In yards across
the lands an anesthesia
clouds the eyes and masks

their apprehension. In homes
across the globe a snow
of cheap commotion

envelops talk and art
and paltry stories starring
in the morning paper.

Cigarettes, drumbeats,
sounds of the patched jugular
cross and flare and feather

into one winged space or else
another. But this retired's
likeness will one day

overlook a Roman hill
that overlooks the Tiber's
briny tide. And over lattes

under swaying palms,
watching boats and planes
make their *via dolorosa*

within the sticky clinic
that is the world,
hammered hearts

will treat themselves
to sun and town and then
a cathedral's timeless weather.

# April 15, 2013

Our taxes paid or almost,
two bombs went off in Boston
and the runners, deafened, staggered
from the blast and their disbelief.

All across America the internet
lit up, a race to relive the outrage,
a contest to connect the latest data
with the never-happens-here,

the did-you-hear with the
we-don't-fear. Over and over
we saw the smoke. We saw
the grainy rush-away, the drilled

rush-toward. We heard
three killed, limbs severed.
We heard the suited speakers
and recognized their speeches.

Two bombs went off in Boston—
while in Zabul Province,
an entire family's seven dead,
thirty bodies spread across Iraq.

# Make a Difference!
## —*a villanelle to commencement speakers everywhere*

Tonight, fatigue's grim flower unfurls,
but Gandhi, gunned down, had this to say:
"Be the change you wish to see in the world."

Oh? Even when casting before swine my pearls,
every action seems absurd, and all the day—
and tonight—fatigue's grim flower unfurls?

Even though, in my disgust, I'd hurl
the grenades myself, I should, anyway,
be the change I wish to see in the world?

What about how resolve just sways and swirls?
What about colleagues countering, "Let's pray"?
Especially then fatigue's grim flower unfurls,

failure feels relentless, all fervor whirls.
But still I'm to spin—on these feet of clay—
this *Be the change you wish to see in the world*?

The global Bottom Line confirms *I'm* the churl
and binds me with a twist to the old cliché:
tonight, fatigue's grim flower's unfurled
*by* the change I'd wished to see in the world.

# Surreal Expulsion
## —for Marjory Stoneman Douglas High School

Fourteen chairs loiter, emptied, no young bodies
adjusting for the next lesson, hand-raising,
class-clown antic, contemplative talk, pat show
of teen contempt, rhythm beaten with pencil, palm,
bouncing knee, jouncing heal, wise-crack, step
in the impossible problem never to be solved.
Instead, more of the same news, the same vows
taxiing the hellish hallways of feigned intention
but never taking off—the same dazed moments
of the dead. Perhaps their freed spirits now see
through the coal-black tunnel of some eternity
right into the next school's beehive of victims.
Perhaps they still shadow their three steady mentors
who stood staunch ground in the slow-motion flow
of high-speed ammo. The clip of names shoots holes
clean through law's callous gut—

                        Aaron, Helena, and Alex,
Carmen, Peter, Cara, Chris, and Meadow,
           Scott, Alaina, Martin, Alyssa, and Nick,
Jamie, Luke, Gina, and "Guac" Joaquin—

                               whose roll call
claims only an absurd third of a minute, while
their totaled lives witnessed nearly 5 thousand
wheels of the moon through some 75 trillion miles.
But unlike the pull of that implacable moon,
the glib fever of 'prayers and condolences' can't
turn the tide of memory's radiating its fixed

fissures scored by shards of glass and bone.
Here, we're left to settle the moonscape of Too Late
for those whose expelled footsteps befuddle us.
And lauding immortality soothes no better. We
know we relax at our children's peril, run rash risk
of shoring up the open/closed-carry-frenzied fight,
take false hope in the bundles of white-washed bills.
Anthony Borges took five bullets to shield twenty
surviving friends, sacrificed his soccer stardom
because somehow he knew what he had to do.
His lacerated back and shattered femur scream
in a language we now must teach across America.

# Notes

"Upon Recognizing Yesterday's 'Well-Meaning' Poem Was Still as Paternalistic as Ever": On January 22, 2017, the massive Women's March on Washington to protest the inauguration of Donald Trump was supported by similar marches all over the world.

"The 27th of January, 2017": This poem is after Galway Kinnel's "The 26th of December" and is dated a week after the inauguration of Donald Trump.

"Brit Lit Weighs In": A true *cento*, which in Latin means "patchwork," is made up entirely of lines from other sources. In this case: *Beowulf*, Chaucer, *Everyman*, Spenser, Shakespeare, Herrick, Marvell, Milton, Dryden, Pope, Johnson, Gray, Burns, Blake, Wordsworth, Coleridge, Byron, Shelley, Keats, Tennyson, Browning, Arnold, Swinburne, Hopkins, Hardy, Yeats, Eliot, Housman, Auden, Thomas, Larkin.

"A – maze – d": Merle Rosen (1949-2017), an American artist practicing in Cincinnati, Ohio, exhibited in the U.S. and abroad.

"Imagining a Demise": This poem is after Pablo Neruda's "Youth."

"Pain, No Gain": This is a 'found poem' whose text is courtesy, with permission, of Patti and Warren Finke, Team Oregon.

"Pope Goes, a Weasel?": Pope Benedict XVI abdicated in 2013, 598 years after Gregory XII did so to end the so-called Papal Schism.

"April 15, 2013": On this date the deadly terrorist bombing at the Boston Marathon finish line occurred, as well as multiple terrorist car bombings in Afghanistan and Iraq, which went largely unnoticed in the U.S.

"Surreal Expulsion": On February 14, 2018, a shooting at Marjory Stoneman Douglas High School in Parkland, Florida, killed seventeen and wounded seventeen. The perpetrator, 19-year-old Nikolas Cruz, was identified by witnesses and arrested. He owned at least ten guns, seven of which were purchased legally.

# Acknowledgments

Many thanks to the publications that brought these poems into the world, some in slightly different versions:

*Bullets into Bells:* "Surreal Expulsion"

*Dunes Review:* "Lines Concocted While Waiting to Catch a Certain Bent Blue Note in Jimi Hendrix's Second Guitar Solo of 'Voodoo Child (Slight Return)' Recorded Live at London's Albert Hall, February 24, 1969"

*Galway Review* (Ireland): "An Assembly of God"

*Pif Magazine:* "The 27$^{th}$ of January, 2017" and "Imagining a Demise" (as "Prof")

*Poetry Quarterly:* "First Light"

*Rise Up Review:* "April 15, 2013"

*Sheila-Na-Gig:* "Penny" and "A – maze – d"

*SurVision: "Wedged, Continued"*

*Tuck:* "Make a Difference!"

*Typishly:* "Dream at Wits' End"

*Unbroken:* "New Year Cliché'd"

*Unlost Journal:* "Pain, No Gain" and "Brit Lit Weighs In"

*Writers Resist:* "OK, Here's What We Do: An Allegory" and "Upon Recognizing That Yesterday's 'Well-Meaning' Poem Was Still as Paternalistic as Ever"

## *—Additionally—*

"April 15, 2013" is reprinted in *The Poeming Pigeon: In the News.*

"Make a Difference!" is reprinted in *Writers Resist.*

"Penny" and "A – maze – d" (as "a::::maze::::d") are reprinted in *The Ekphrastic Review.*

"The 27th of January, 2017" is reprinted in *Sisyphus.*

"Upon Recognizing That Yesterday's 'Well-Meaning' Poem Was Still as Paternalistic as Ever" is also anthologized in *Writers Resist: The Anthology 2018.* Eds. Kit-Bacon Gressitt and Sara Marchant. Running Wild Press, 2018.

"A – maze – d" (as "a::::maze::::d") is also reprinted in *Blue Ash Review*'s chapbook tribute to Merle Rosen.

# Praise for *Surreal Expulsion*

D.R. James' *Surreal Expulsion* does not close itself to the events of our historical moment, but invites them into the "fortress of language" to work their "eccentric twisting in the inexplicable path." In such a short collection lies a range of forms—prose poems, a villanelle, a cento, a sonnet, as well as free verse—that push language to fathom this twenty-first-century life of ours: deep political divisions in the national "family," near-routine mass shootings in schools, consumerist imagination bleeding into a literary one that we only thought was impervious. With textured lines and crackling diction, these poems register our nervous collective pulse.

~ Ellen McGrath Smith, editor of *Bullets into Bells*, author of *Scatter, Feed* and *Nobody's Jackknife*

The poems in *Surreal Expulsion* are both topical and wise as they address the human condition, and they deftly walk the line between gravitas and levity. Some of that levity comes from the very apparent love D.R. James has for the sound of language and the potential for word play that arises from the making of meaning. As intellectual exercises, these poems wake the mind and ask us to consider our place among the masses; as verbal *amuse-bouches*, they feel good in the mouth and ask to be savored.

~ Sonia Greenfield, editor of *Rise Up Review*, author of *American Parable* and *Boy with a Halo at the Farmer's Market*

*Surreal Expulsion* is aptly titled. Many of these poems serve as chimeric rejections of the past or the fearful future, the foregone, the despicable, the uncertain. Read them and you'll discover harsh metaphors of childhood, of a "small-bodied boy" who terrorizes a puppy, another with "naked legs like sprung sausage curls," "the perfect girl straining to witness her big brother's totemic ecstasy." You'll envision dreams, or perhaps nightmares, of the natural world—a "remote ocean boiling away its underwater flora and fauna" —and its institutions— a "bellied, brimstoning minister" in whose churchyard a "lacy little girl in shiny shoes / comes fluttering among the unsung mothers and, / still young, postpones payment of her fated dues."

But the poems of resistance pluck an activist's strings most intimately. They compose a requiem for a nation we thought we knew, rich with horror— "a certain absurdity … blurting like boils," "War that mushrooms undiminished" —and scant of hope— "optimism will seem a stretch." Read them and you'll find not a eulogy, no celebration of remembered heroes, but a sorrowful, wrenching threnody. Cry out, if you must, rend your clothes, gnash your teeth to stubs, lament like a Scotch-Irish ballad, but they will have you know: these abominations are ours, "in a language we now must teach across America." They are a call to action. How will you respond?

~ Kit-Bacon Gressitt, publisher and a founding editor of
*Writers Resist* (online) and *Writers Resist Anthology 2018*

# About the Author

D. R. James's seven previous poetry collections include *If god were gentle* (Dos Madres Press 2017), *Since Everything Is All I've Got* (March Street Press 2011), and the chapbooks *Split-Level* and *Why War* (both Finishing Line Press 2017 and 2014).

James earned an MA in English and Composition from the University of Iowa and an MFA in Creative Writing from Pacific University and has been teaching writing, literature, and peace-making at Hope College for 34 years. He lives in the woods outside of Saugatuck, Michigan, with his wife, psychotherapist Suzy Doyle, and between them they have six grown children, four grandchildren, two cats, and one wondrous life.

# About The Poetry Box®

The Poetry Box® was founded by Shawn Aveningo Sanders & Robert R. Sanders, who wholeheartedly believe that every day spent with the people you love, doing what you love, is a moment in life worth cherishing. Their boutique press celebrates the talents of their fellow artisans and writers through professional book design and publishing of individual collections, as well as their flagship literary journal, *The Poeming Pigeon*.

Feel free to visit the online bookstore (thePoetryBox.com), where you'll find more titles including:

*Keeping It Weird: Poems & Stories of Portland, Oregon*

*The Way a Woman Knows* by Carolyn Martin

*Giving Ground* by Lynn M. Knapp

*Broadfork Farm* by Tricia Knoll

*Psyche's Scroll* by Karla Linn Merrifield

*November Quilt* by Penelope Scambly Schott

*14: Antologia del Sonoran* by Christopher Bogart

*Shrinking Bones* by Judy K. Mosher

*Epicurean Ecstasy* by Cynthia Gallaher

*Many Sparrows* by donnarkevic

and more . . .

www.ingramcontent.com/pod-product-compliance
Lightning Source LLC
LaVergne TN
LVHW090040080526
838202LV00046B/3893